Also by Carmen Germain

Living Room, Earth

These Things I Will Take with Me

The Old Refusals

LIFE DRAWING

LIFE DRAWING

poems

Carmen Germain

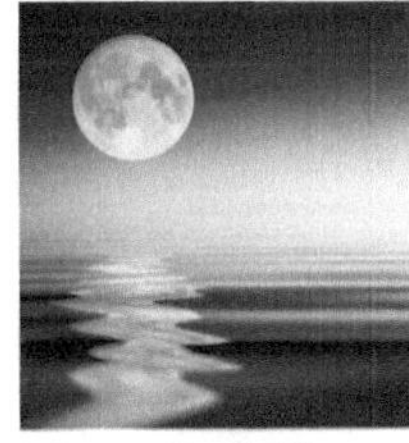

MoonPath Press

Copyright © 2022 Carmen Germain
All rights reserved.

No part of this publication may be reproduced, distributed, or
transmitted in any form or by any means whatsoever without
written permission from the publisher, except in the case of
brief excerpts for critical reviews and articles. All inquiries
should be addressed to MoonPath Press.

Poetry
ISBN 978-1-936657-68-1

Cover art by Carmen Germain, *Man with Green Shirt*,
acrylic on canvas,
photographed by Eric Neurath

Author photo by Laura Fox

Book design by Tonya Namura, using Avaline Script (display) and
Corporate A Condensed Pro (text).

MoonPath Press, an imprint of Concrete Wolf Poetry Series,
is dedicated to publishing the finest poets
living in the U.S. Pacific Northwest.

MoonPath Press
PO Box 445
Tillamook, OR 97141

MoonPathPress@gmail.com

http://MoonPathPress.com

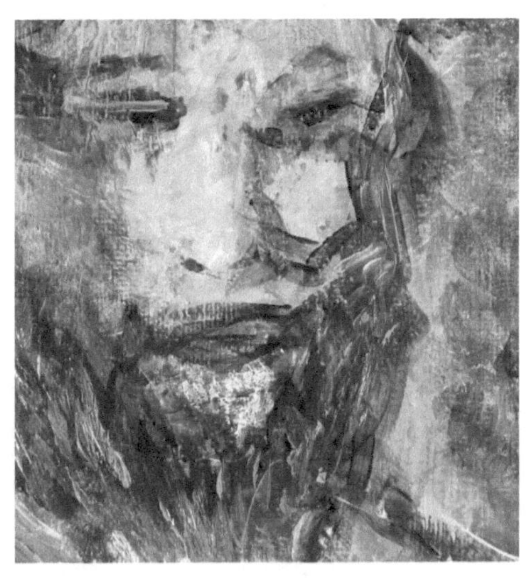

For Tom, in all ways

Acknowledgments

In gratitude to the journals in which these poems first appeared, some in slightly different form:

Cider Press Review: "Thorn on a Riff of Sweet"

Cold Mountain Review: "Some adults with insomnia"

Crosscurrents: "The Dam Tourist" and "The Evil Counsellors, The Despots"

Literary Accents: "Infinitesimal the distance"

Northwind Art Center, Port Townsend, Washington: Ekphrastic event: "Red-tailed Hawk"

The Madrona Project, Volume II, Number 1 *Keep a Green Bough*: Voices from the Heart of Cascadia: "Butterbur (and Wild Pansy)"

The Madrona Project, Volume II, Number 2 *Human Communities in Wild Places*: "Brother Rat"

In Appreciation

A few of these poems in early stages were critiqued by Sally
Albiso (1950-2019) who left us her brave and clear-eyed
poetry. She is dearly missed. Thank you to Phyllis van Holland
for images of brilliantly colored visual art on dark days and
for helping me understand that personal poems can speak
a universal language. Holly J. Hughes was invaluable as we
workshopped some of these poems; her insight regarding
which poems worked best in what order solved some difficult
problems. I extend much gratitude to Charlotte Gould Warren
for bringing a finely tuned and sixth-sense poet's eye to this
manuscript; her careful attention was greatly appreciated.
Thank you to Jim Bertolino, upper Mississippi River *paesano*, for
his encouragement. Many thanks to the poetry community of
this region for their books and poems, an on-going inspiration.
MoonPath Press graphic designer Tonya Namura deserves
thanks for her work in designing beautiful books. A special
bouquet of foxgloves and wild tiger lilies for Lana Hechtman
Ayers, managing editor of MoonPath Press, for her dedication to
poets of the Pacific Northwest.

Table of Contents

LIFE DRAWING

don't be afraid, and don't try to make it pretty

–Vincent van Gogh

I.

Needle Song

unbleached broderie anglaise

I think of her one hundred years in the grave,
fingerbones skilled in oblivion. Fine linen cutwork
traced and snipped by scissors through afternoons

while her children schooled or slept. Wash done.
Chicken butchered and dashed in boiling water
in the henyard, pin feathers scorched. Sweet corn

hoed, joe-pye weed chopped to roots. House
set to rhythms of oval eyelets. Maybe it was desire
for something so useless it couldn't wipe or rub

or clean or dust or wrap anything dead or living.
How he'd say, "Why do you tear holes in good cloth?"
as she worked running stitches and pierced centers

with a stiletto folded back along the cut. Maybe she
hung it in her window, dawn blooming vermilion
as she rose from her sleep, chosen by light.

Red-Tailed Hawk

*after Chilled in Early Morning Sun
by Wanda Mawhinney*

Emile Zola said, "Art is a corner of nature
seen through a temperament." Here
it's a scumble of cloud and sgraffito
catching us in the scour and sweep

the way years ago we hiked Mesa Verde
while wind rocked plateau nights,
stars a blaze of yellow yarrow.
Everything belonged—

blue work shirt snapping rope
we strung in spruce, rock art
scratched in a box canyon, how the day
bled into the next where we

watched a red-tailed hawk soar
a thermal. When we saw it again,
we were not the same people,
and it was not the same hawk.

Before Time

Summer 2020

Stop! You are so beautiful!–like Faust
trying to clinch the moment, I crush blossoms
between wax paper and the *Riverside Shakespeare.*
Foxgloves teeter at the ends of stalks,
hummingbirds war for sugar.
Stringing webs, spiders spin in huckleberry.
A centipede curls green in the flute of a leaf of salal.
Dangling its faux fruit, the Oregon grape.
Ten days later I lift the weight and find
violet's shriveled to punk, and where it's damp,
mold on mauve leaves. The highway's booming,
tourists from Texas and California and Ohio,
Florida and Arizona and Iowa hauling boats and trailers.
Lapdogs yapping in RVs called *Wilderness* and *Solitude,*
kayaks clapped on roofs of SUVs. In town
people drink beer two feet apart in acid-yellow light,
protestors 100 miles from here maced again last night.
Monday's your heart echo, another turn this summer.

It's begun, earth slowly tipping away from its star.
At 9 pm, you say, "See! The days are getting shorter,"
the way we felt that year in the Four Corners,
sleeping in the back of the 122S. In a cliff dwelling
I splayed my hand in a woman's handprint
from the eleventh century, my fingerbones
in place of hers. How she worked black-on-red clay
coiled for a pot, pinching the rim. I want to say
it was a sacred moment, the time before everything
happened. How she wore a polished turquoise
pendant, blue-green light glazing red rock.

Haircut Song

after "Cutting My Husband's Hair on Labor Day"
by Holly J. Hughes

Lost somewhere in this house
is your ponytail the barber handed me
in a plastic bag in Sacramento.
You wanted to get your hair cut,
ropey length flopping in the way
of working on the car or stir frying.
Then because trips to the barber
cost $2, I got the job, chopped
your hair 70s style.

They now seem deranged, those rockers,
names like Pacific Gas & Electric
and? Question Mark & The Mysterians,
faces sneering out of frizzy shrubs.
Keith Richards, haystack on his head,
Deep Purple, hair like spaghetti gone gummy.

Over decades
I've snipped your umber waves,
and sideburns begun as muttonchops
have gone the way of whitewalls.

You won't let me clip wisps floating
your crown as I tell you of childhood
Sundays, how gainfully bored
I counted strands plastered across pates
of old men kneeling, but you won't be
wheedled either, check my work
in the mirror, won't let me trim
your eyebrows' wangling wires.
I'll keep rubbing lotion

on the cleared runway
of your scalp where gnats
glide in summer
to the gleaming invitation—
shiny smooth, no bramble and bush.
No tangled understory.

After Your Heart Attack, I Return to This Poem

'66 122S Volvo Wagon

We don't call the junkyard yet
even though the hood's glazed with lichen
and jammed, wrench locked in the latch,
tires slowly breaking from beads.
From California to Maine
while you drove, I read Dante,
preferring the roar of Hell
to the rose of Paradise:

> *He carried me to Minos: eight times round*
> *His scabby back the monster coiled his tail,*
> *Then biting it in rage he pawed the ground–*

bouncing logging roads in British Columbia
to the Yellowknife. Between rocks and trees
on the coastal route north the moon danced
mountain roads silvered in headlights–
before air tags, no one could find you
if you didn't want to be found.

Creatures of a certain time
roaming place to place with paper maps,
we knew it wouldn't always be this way,
easy to work the finicky clutch, shifting
gears as though conducting a symphony.

People pushed notes under the wipers–
would we sell this classic car?
How we'd wax the finish to a creamy gleam.

Cancer of rust, they call it, for all things
erode and break down,
hood and trunk lid and fenders, roof
with its pool of rain,
and like someone weary from life's
back-and-forth, the transmission's stuck
in reverse, wheels digging in gravel:
I will not be abandoned
with the mice and the weeds.

Fingerprint Correspondence

My first supervisor had never heard of Steinbeck,
how she'd circle my typos in red, my little flames of ineptitude
where I misfired codes and crimes in two-inch columns
of police dockets in the clerk-typist pool,
damning the wrong person to Felony Elude or Burglary III
if my fingers slid the wrong keys.

Before DNA testing and big data,
analysts rode swirls of prints all day, crouching
over drafting tables, squinting at eddies of the alleged
and convicted. I imagined stories
for mugshots, tried to match crimes to codes,
eyes of the accused wide as frying pans

while peace talks slowed between the crosses row on row.
Sirening through town, the president's motorcade snapped flags
on each fin. All day analysts plotted twists and whirls
of fingerprints like radiologists practiced in galaxies of cells.

At 5:00 p.m. White people boarded buses to Maryland and Virginia.
At 5:00 p.m. Black people boarded buses into DC,
domestic and maintenance workers home
past SE shops, barred windows, and iron doors
to more cooking and cleaning.

Grapes of Wrath, I told her.

On Grant and Green

I pause at the Stella Bakery where cannoli aches
to be stuffed with fresh ricotta
and chocolate, where pizzelle thin as lace
hums with anise. Broadway barkers wheel and deal
     strip shows for conventioneers,
City Lights a bright blade, and the beat museum

across the street like a vault
walled against the world, blown-up
black-and-white Ginsberg and Corso
and Kerouac. Forty years ago Ferlinghetti–
     "My Cadillac...should I drive it?
might put a scratch on it...should I take a cab?"

So ride the #32 straight to North Beach
and Chinatown, red dragons and dim sum.
Cross hills downtown to the city center,
Museum of Modern Art–
     Picasso and de Kooning,
swagger and insomnia and The Woman.

For Norm Pierce's record store
on Page and Haight, take #17, stand reeling
as a man talks to himself, the only one
not yelling in his cell.
     Haight/Ashbury–
where a young woman leaps on the sidewalk,

thrusts hips in the joy of her body's roil. Years ago,
my hair a rope of copper silk sweeping past my waist,
I waited for a green light, and a man waiting there, too,
Afro framing his face, asked
     if he could touch my braid,
and I said *Sure* in the imperceptible shift toward less night.

Since then, the years have mashed together like people
on a crowded bus. My hair's chopped and shading to gray.
How it felt, that living coil imagined in his hand.
How we stood with each other, and no one was afraid.

Yelp of a boy diving in water,

steam of August heat
warming the cove on the farmland lake,
the drop into cold. I see you now
in tornado weather, skinny kid, droop
of jeans off your hips.

Once when you ran away,
we fanned out on the country road
and pretended not to see the ditch
where you crouched, better for us to circle
and bring home our prey.

Our taunts about your bony legs,
ribcage curving your lump of heart where
blundering we found our sibling victim.

Brother, I rummage things of childhood
to find lost blessing.

One summer you uncovered a gopher drowned
in its tunnel, sealed the body in a jar
and kept it for weeks, discovering
the raw goods of biology,
the stew submerging fur and bone.

How I couldn't look away either,
learned you and I were the animals
who know ahead of time
how much there is to lose.

Under the roof of dusk,

horse on a rope in the fog,
the rancher slogs the field verge,
river shifting to moonrise.
I remember another moon,

gazing with my mother.
How we had nothing to say
to each other, woman
and girl who never touched.

Then she raised her hand
and stroked my head
in a time before I knew
such poetry in the world.

II.

Pictorial, Loaded

helping my mother shelve used books
donated by ex-pats to the American Legion,
Lake Chapala, Jalisco

Blue stickers on spines of fiction, red on history,
yellow on self-help. Green for recipes, pink for romance,
the mass market kind, most popular genre in the world.
This is not *Love in the Time of Cholera* or *Kristin Lavansdatter*,
which Mother has just finished on her Kindle, but I will not
monkey-wrench as I sort piles dumped by the homesick

moving back to the States or by a relative cleaning out closets.
She says someone came in and rearranged all books
alphabetically by author, colors of the rainbow careening,
everyone flummoxed: Ambrose's Lewis and Clark expedition
propped next to Jane Austen. But easy to tell if it's Harlequin
or a knock-off by looking at cover art—

man and woman reeling from deep kissing on a beach:
The Accidental Island. Woman in bustier and tight jeans,
posed against man (he glistens, well-oiled), his hands
hovering deliciously near her crotch: *Caught by the Cowboy*.
At eighty, my mother's quick, glances at paperbacks,
categorizes, peels sticker sheets, slaps down. Where it gets

confusing—the covers with nuanced sex: décolletage
decorated with an orchid or a single bloom not unlike
Georgia O'Keeffe's *Black Iris*. Titles suspicious, budget
publishers. "Just open it anywhere," my mother advises.
"If it says, 'she spread her legs in ecstasy,' it's Romance."
I remember a poem by a fifty-year-old in a long marriage

speaking of the joy of intimacy with her husband,
words like "boneless creatures," "starburst," and
"thick white towels," and a student's critique,
"two old people naked in a bathtub was a real turn-off,"
decrying her yellow silk vest, red cowboy boots—
how she shouldn't dress that way, woman her age.

Oh, we're like crows feasting on the ancient crop
of criticism. How when I saw Grace Hartigan's photo
in her eighth decade—New York School artist
of great appetites, all those husbands and legions of lovers—
I deplored her Barbara Bush string of pearls and navy knit
dress, her snowy hairdo blushed with blue.

Today I shovel one-step, two-step rhythm

even though I did this yesterday and the day before
the day before and still the snow will not rain.
I'm restless with this clotted cream under gray sky.

How I need a green-cheeked Amazon parrot,
black eyes ringed with gold. Orange graffiti
on a passing freight, copper snake in the bathtub.

Can of red paint kicked over, lemons in a blue bowl
in a kitchen in Mexico. Banana trees and birds
of paradise. Two bony horses grazing beside

a stone wall, cool before the rains. Bursts
of bougainvillea, donkey with a load of straw.
Make it a dream, this car mired in snow

pinning tires up to hubs. A dream, this thawing
and freezing until my shovel no longer bites
but bends. Plows scraping the country roads

through the ruts, three feet of snow curling eaves
like fists reaching for windows to break winter
into the house...avalanches off the metal roof

where we glance up whenever leaving. A dream,
my mother's handwriting in a sketchbook,
"behind = detrás, in front = delantero."

Incantatory, the Whistle's *Oh, Oh, Oh*

> *East of Malta, flash of freights sudden*
> *on rails in the night, jolt of wind*
> *when two bodies almost meet.*

We'd touched on death so casually as though
it were not listening and standing near—
agreed ninety might be enough
before everything went to hell.

I cut her a slice of ruby rhubarb pie,
gazed out windows in a July that will never
come again. She flew home.
I caught the train back to mountains and sea,

but this is not an elegy.

She'd never approve, couldn't endure
weepy endearments.

When my father lost his footing in this world,
she said, "If you cry, I'll cry, and I won't cry
until he's gone," and while I wept,
she kept her back to me
in the blue stucco hospital open to wasps,
cries from the market across the street,
its beaded jaguars and green painted fish.

How I heard flutes of the knife sharpeners,
ethereal mountain tones I'd never heard before.

But her week in dying she kept secret,
wished not to have us board planes,
converge on the house, grown children
dropping grief around her bed.

Knowing nothing, thousands of miles north
I chopped scotch broom and blackberry cane,
wondered at thrush and robins
past breeding singing mid-day—
chorus in the maple and cedar and hemlock.

If I believed in anything, I'd think they sang
to spirit her away. *Good Lord,* she'd say.

It was only birds singing.

Infinitesimal the distance

between before and after
how a travel trailer veers

off its towpath into my lane
then passes ghost-like

through the windshield
before correcting

Thorn on a Riff of Sweet

In Altamira, Don De Sautuola
heard "Look, Papa, *oxen*," and
Neolithic bison thundered
back into the world. What is given

astonishes:
unripe Himalayan blackberries hanging
a precipice of April,
in May, green as Chinese

porcelain. Cochineal crimson
in July, the indigo of August
bursting into sugar among bees.
If I stumbled among this cane-

heavy fruit, the ravine's bramble
drop would plunge me into
the deep mouth of September,
fermenting a terrifying wine

as silent as the cave in France
before torchlight, and breath
of beasts held still
waiting to be found.

Life Drawing

Gazing at portraits it's not hard to see
how Old Masters painted vanity pictures,
keeping wise, knowing what could kill—
emperors dashing off heads the way

juncos in meadows snap blossoms from vetch.
Painters didn't draw true to life if the duchess
dripped double chins and umber daubs couldn't hide
how she plumped. Under sugar (gnarly pose

of some lord, his wolfhound heavy-lidded
watching proceedings) was salt, hours grinding
pigment, stained hands revealing who was master,
who was maker living by art. I think of Alice Neel,

still painting at eighty, how she shows
what we live toward if we live long enough.
Doesn't sugarcoat saggy thighs, belly's swag.
Breasts flaccid as the bags between legs of old men.

Mouth straight-lined in concentration, she holds
a brush in her right hand, rag in her left.
She's looking in a mirror, head tipped up,
but gazing straight at us, too—so we know

what we're getting into. How she leans forward
on the chair of vertical stripes,
and she's on the edge, not sinking but solid,
pulse brushed red into her jowls

for skin tone, the way Rubens blushed models,
but she tells us other ways to know the body,
green on her shoulder as though she belongs
to earth. Her first self-portrait, and her first nude.

You know she'd never say *I'm eighty years young,*
would never join The Best Is Yet to Be Club.
This, she'd say, *is human. True to life. Salt.*

Nothing being equal

how soon the light's broken—
meat clawed then gnawed to bone.
River, big leaf maple, licorice fern,

nighthawks scratching nests in gravel.
Long grass thick with wood ticks,
and this cougar kill, bluebottle born.

Wildfire, tornado, earthquake, war—
reporters tolling the disaster, sky bland as *nice*.
Birds glancing down, flying faster.

~

Wearing the hated word "widow"
one month out, she deleted his name
from their life savings account

and with the teller's chittering
"Have a great rest of the day,"
leaped 90,000 miles away.

Beast

for Jack Gilbert

You couldn't know
How the brain
a disease of nature
fiery poet
when I dropped you
How you asked
and in my mind
loved ones somber
How you wished
cracking your neck.
allowing you
this violent surprise.
"Imagine being

its pouncing.
consumes itself
destroying light
squinting fox-like
off at the airport.
What's your ideal death?
the usual bed scene
near my sedated meat.
some stalking puma
Annihilation at once
to live until just
How people would say,
devoured by a beast!"

After "Nightmare"

How it's possible
to live in the world and not smell its char
            —Sally Albiso, "Nightmare"

Mephisto, too, has a downward leap of faith at times,
like headlights dying on a mountain curve, even though
ninety percent of people say they believe in him
and in the competitors Evil and Good. But sometimes
confidence desires a perfect score.

He's never visited me in nightmare the way he entered
your dream, Sally, squatting on your chest to gather
blandishments. But I hear the night terrors of my husband,
how he mangles conversation in his throat.
I've stopped shaking him awake. He never remembers
the cargo weighting his sleep.

And mornings I sometimes feel the "was" before "is"
when I'm not yet fully awake, birdsong breaking
first light. Along the way, Mephisto wants to be
in the details, loots our lives for his pleasure.

I think of Dupree Bolton, a tape cut in prison,
the only existing sound of his solo trumpet. Slogging
"John's Tune," laboring behind time, the convict band's wary
of stretching out, but Bolton's gift could've taken him
anywhere. His riff breaks free, breaching like a stunned bird,
wings beating against the odds. But once outside,

he scored heroin instead of music. How are we to know
what might've been? Maybe years later someone heard
a bebop "Katanga" on a street in San Francisco,
followed the sound. Met Bolton on a scrap of cardboard
playing devil-may-care, and better the one you know.

Día de los Muertos

In the folk-art museum
the All-Souls altar–

my face suddenly
in an oval mirror

banked with marigolds
among the sugar bones

Choose Your Own

for Lucky Thompson

Your gift was honed from woodshedding, hermit
of undertow, hermit despising false
gold, sound of money clinking hand to hand
only for pop jazz, your music a dark star.
How he babbles who trivializes art—
"Heigh Ho Jazzoids!" Hermits need solitude,
the cadence of breathing the only sound.
Your music's fire-cracked seed, gift rising
from its burning. "Choose your own," you said.
Producers shape taste, and it needs telling: art's
built from blood and bone and soul. You wagered
your life to this one truth, its mystery
asleep with boats and rain...abandoned art
of compromise, your hermit-haunted sound.

His Walden

How ignorant I am fighting some poem
while your youngest son, world traveler–
lies dying in his terrible illness,
what contains his fire not world enough.

How I twist language hoping to see something...
"Moments ago sun breached mountains"
or "Sun shatters dawn in the mountains"
or "Morning, sun strikes the same mountains"
moving from past to present, as obsessed as Flaubert courting

his commas. On my bookshelves, nature poets,
l-a-n-g-u-a-g-e poets. Lyric or narrative or lyric-narrative,
neoformal or steampunk poets, words alive listening
while I plod in a circle like a sad-harnessed pony

at a country fair, no sleek horse trotting beyond the gate.
I work this way for hours while your son dies in a cabin
by a forest lake–"his Walden"–the only place he wants
to be on this earth. Sunrise a spark tipping
Mount Storm King, longing to be seen.

Like Colored Glass: A Cento

Fully furnished home
On Lake Sutherland,
Large deck with lots of sun.
Sept. 15 - May 1st.
No smoking/poets.
          –Peninsula Daily News
          Port Angeles, Washington

Poets, of course, butcher nothing but their own ideas,
and sometimes, when the living can endure their losses

no longer, words can do this. Out of the hush and rustlings
come noises that seem left poking up after some immense

subtraction: we hear a jade bell's laughter and think
it laughs at us. Yet why not say what happened?

Pray for the grace of accuracy Vermeer gave
to the sun's illumination and the gray sunflower

poised against the sunset, crackly bleak
and dusty with the smut and smog and smoke.

Ah, sunflower, weary of time, who counts the steps
of the sun. Beyond the soggy garden, two kayaks

float across mild clear water. A red sun stains the lake
like colored glass   autumn winter spring summer.

III.

So much of war

is waiting for war. All through childhood I heard
his stories, how troops from Ordnance
stole copper pipe for hooch they drank

too green,

long lines the next day for the latrine.

Pranks and good times like summer camp
for farm boys ten million miles from home.

But forty years later my father sat in the dark,
customers gone for the day, cars masked for painting,

dents pounded out, the side-swiped and collisions
no one wanted to scrap, grief grinding in.

~

Because I ask, he shows me a map
of Papua New Guinea, points to the highlands.

"So many dead, they loaded them in 6 x 6s.

It really bothered some guys,
but it really didn't bother me."

~

Big-hip Holsteins, shit smell of them—
how he hated it as a boy,
their inner tube tongues lolling
salt licks, how they never wanted barn
in fall or pasture in spring, never wanted
anything but pleasure of cud or spurt
of milk in the pail.

How he loved cars—
fine ticking of an engine well made, the way
wheels bounced over ruts on the farm,
feel of steering under his hands.

The war got him out, put his mind on tanks
and trucks to keep them running.

~

He tells me about a photograph sent home.
A Japanese begging for his life.
How infantry shot the others.

All you could see were legs of soldiers
like a circle caging the prisoner.

Crouching the way all of us hold on,
lives famous only to ourselves.

Egg Logic

Worker wasps, patiently social,
swirl the hive of chamber cells
for all of it to start again—

hunt living meat of spiders
and moths to feed offspring
of the Queen, daughters

that'll never be mothers.
There's never any outrage,
never any brighter dreams.

By June the world's
all egg logic: life writhing
in paper nests of pulp

from old posts and fences,
siding of cedar houses
where the Queen, bloated

on her throne
delivers the news...
all of it to start again.

Butterbur (and Wild Pansy)

on a painting by Morris Graves

Pure luminosity, the butterbur, scarlet off-white frothing,
striking and spirited, each stamen's pinpoint of light

in a skyrocket of smoke and noise, the way happiness
like a festival takes over, fireworks staving off darkness

in a barrage of pyrotechnics.

In a translucent bottle, purple-blue petals in five directions,
a wild pansy poses next to this ballistic. It's said violets
grew wherever Orpheus put down his lyre

and I like to think because he honored music so much—

his beautiful song—the viola spread its leaves
to open more to listening.

Three red-orange rosehips

lean forward, alert to the darker tone of these petals,
how men prefer this shade while women, like Persephone,
are drawn to the lighter. Still the butterbur catches me first,

stolid in its bronze vessel. How it thrusts shoulders forward
like someone in charge about to shout orders.

But it's the wild pansy where I keep returning, how it emerges
from milky glass not shrinking, how two leaves rise like hands

to praise such fragile peace.

The Counterfeiters

Good to keep in mind how gallery security closed
lights after hours, and Americana paintings
with Old Masters on loan nodded in darkness,

democracy wobbly as to who's equal

and who isn't. So portraits of Founding Fathers–
the rich will always be with us–Hudson River
School, farm scenes with chaff-blowing plow horses,
proper colonial wives in lace collars, and the red-blushed
beauty attributed to Vermeer hung together. Art forgery's
not new.

Worldwide there's always been plunder,
ancient jewelry fashioned from human bones.

But on my walls *Wild Hair Mountain* by Josie Gray,
and a watercolor bought in Venice from a street artist–
man rowing canals in the greeny dawn.
An India ink on paper, *Woman Dancing*, too.

While no forger I believe ever chanced a crooked print
of Kollwitz's *No More War*, picture envy
        needing a sweet piece neutral over the couch,
not a woman lifting her arms to cry "Enough!"

Van Meegeren disdained Sunday painters,
scoured shops in Amsterdam for 17th century discard,
ground cracked
from brushing lean over fat.

All those sour faces of ancestors no one cared
to remember. How he scored surfaces
with caustic soda, vanished images by sanding,
and painted in the style of Vermeer,
bringing crazed work out where he rubbed
ashes in breaks of glazes. Studied
how the famous artist
caught the character of the human heart, what counts
and what doesn't–

sneered van Gogh was only
finger painting.

How the forger copied over-the-shoulder
the face in Vermeer's *The Girl with a Glass of Wine*
where a penis-talking suitor was seducing her.

How van Meegeren pimped
the tipsy, smiling girl, called her
the Delft master's own.

The Fixed Stars

> *Why, I ask myself, shouldn't the shining*
> *dots of the sky be as accessible as the black dots*
> *on the map of France? Just as we take the train*
> *to Tarascon or Rouen, we take death to reach a star.*
> *—Vincent van Gogh to his brother*
> *Theo in a letter, July 1889*

Van Gogh worked with nothing in his belly but milk
and dry bread so he could buy paint, and it's true—
he squeezed tubes on canvas and flowed through his fingers
olive groves, cypress, and wheat fields. The starry night.

When his warder went with him as far as the ravine
of Les Peyroulets, van Gogh saw deep red
and burnt sienna, rosemary and black pine,
strands of fire in the narrow valley downslope,
mid-day sun in the V, and a stream of cerulean
falling, rock face and every living thing:
two women on the trail, each in crimson.

When he left the asylum, some paintings
were abandoned or forgotten in a case in his cell,

maybe a companion piece to the ravine
but painted in morning light, which changes
everything. Sun in the valley citron,
and in shadow, rock face purple and rich blue,
rosemary emerald and russet gold. Path empty,
and the music of yellow warblers, his favorite
color, that kind of hope.

How the boy who found the pictures
showed them to his friend—

"What shall we do with them?"

"We could use them as targets,"

and they propped *Les Pevroulets in Morning Sun*
and shot it full of holes.

Maybe van Gogh would've said the profane is no less
profound than the sacred—
only more wounded.

IV.

The Evil Counsellors, The Despots

for Eugenia Ginzburg
Journey into the Whirlwind

1. Ways Out, Autumn 1937

Tell your husband you're dead.
He'll order a black-bordered notice
for the papers. Then no one can arrest him
for lack of vigilance, living with you,
lives crackling like static from a radio
slipped off its station.

Wait until night, pull a scarf
over your head, catch the train
to Pokrovskoye. There's a cottage
with fifteen apple trees.
Bake bread with peasant women—
you're too thin from waiting.
Build meat on your bones with pirozhki and ham.

Or lose your Party card and be expelled for fecklessness.
They'll forget about you, so many apostates
to excommunicate. Flee to Kazakhstan,
live among lamb, ewe, and ram.

Or don't tell your husband
so he won't betray you with his eyes.
Wrap soap and comb in a newspaper,
go to Gypsies in their wandering.
Learn to melt into southern forests,
night draping you where men in silk
slap guitars and women know how to run.

Or keep your husband and give birth
to one more orphan.

2. Black Lake, Winter 1938

Gorky—
once a stone market town where peasants vended
watermelon, baskets of walnuts and almonds.
Chinese in red silk sold black tea, fragrance wheeling
steam from samovars, spigots the carved crowns
of roosters, bright combs among languages of the world—
Asian, European, Persian, Turkish, Tartar, Armenian.
Buttons and bracelets. Topaz, malachite, amethyst.
Music of French concert halls, Tyrolese players
lamenting this or that. Songs of Old Russia.

Imagine anything but your small son's face.
Allow that in, you'll howl like a beast.

"He rolls the executions on his tongue like berries,"
said Mandelstam. Twenty million
like a swarm of stars in a swath of sky.
Corpses shoveled under when land thawed.
And hosed with ice water in the punishment cell
while still alive. Each a woman and each a man. An end
to everything in this world.

3. Car Number 7, Summer 1939

Only the poets
twine music line by line,
breath of being alive.
How you untangle
verse in the freight car,

prisoners among the living.
Reciting from memory
Eugene Onegin,

"His hair cut in the latest mode;
he dined, he danced, he fenced, he rode"

in the same way Homer
conjured the wine-dark sea.

The women in the freight car listen
as land burnt by ice
opens to exile–
how warders trampled
photographs of children
confiscated at Yaroslav station.

And books forbidden, you declaim poetry,
forgetting the rules–
when the train stops at villages
no talking among the human cargo.
Each woman cradling
a mug of water, what the body
needs, human longing
flowing as no water can.

How do you do it–
keep the story going
when guards hearing
the rise and fall of verse
unbolt the door, demand
you pass the contraband?

You recite, and you recite for an hour.

Then the peasant recruit
turns to the other boy recruit,
guns drawn down:

"Think of that, Mishchenko—
every single word by heart."

4. Enemies of the People

Study the cabbage.
Layers folding into layers
of what's peeled back
to reveal the clean heart.

The moon rises like a cabbage
over the things of the world—
a voice answering the voice
buried in snow.
How you're sawing eighteen years

feeding prison stoves,
digging midnight land,
pulling poetry from memory,
nourishing as black bread.

Taiga's sweet September berries,
planks in a hut where a body can rest,
hair threading a fishbone needle.

And earth's grave waiting
for the Georgian.
His bones, too, fugitive as rain.

V.

Bird Theatre

Your money, your money, your money
chattering thin chur, flutes and reeds
ethereal trill, *chickadee deedee*
warble and rattle and burry.
See see you you
look-at-me, look-at-me,
ringing reedy whistle, one-note
two-note, *oh dear me me me*
buzzing descending scold and mew
and the owl's *Who cooks for you?*

We're in the whir of deep-dive
wing-speed whistle, booming air rush
all this hopping and fanning and bobbing
loop flight and courtship feeding
hooting, chasing, drumming, singing.

Could nest our hands
in mosses, rootlets, lichens,
gourds lined with hair and feathers
strung by spider's silk to twigs,
hole smeared with pitch to hinder snakes,
thatch of cattails, trash, and straw,
milkweed stems, willow-seed down.
Cups of shredded bark, caterpillar webs.
Tree flowers, madrone leaves.

Oh, the Year of the Rooster—boasting
and strutting, pecking grain
in its chicken-wire kingdom—

cedar waxwing, goldfinch, swallow,
red-eyed vireo, robin, towhee, black-capped
chickadee. Phoebe and hummingbird

wheeling blackberry cane and seed,
joe-pye weed and gypsy moth, earthworm
and beetle and fruit,

       and Sandhill cranes
in Canada sweeping south,
at rest in fields, roosting
ripples of the Kispiox
by night, circling
valleys for days, dry-pitched
karack karack karack like creaking
of thousands of rusty gates,
the jittery wing launch
to Mexico while the air's still fine,

poplar and birch and rosehips
washed gold in new angles of sun,
the frisson of gathering clouds.

Weekend nights bring out the pickups

when magic some men hoped would happen
doesn't, and the only way to get through
is to race the country roads, radio
blazing, headlights breaking darkness
while bar songs and blues wail stories
no one wants to live but everyone wants
to hear. Like that man tonight raging
past me on the double yellow line.

I think of my neighbor, how he claimed
he was crazy once for what he did,
notched Doug fir low to the ground
in the felling direction. Secret work.
He'd start one off, and they'd ripple
each other like hair on a mountain goat.

How he'd lay a forest on its back, fired
if the outfit he cut for had known what
he was doing. Wild and living
sweet power of muscle,
human engine burning. Creating sky
where there was none, god of light.

Scotch Broom Song

The poets sang praise of evergreen broom
while someone longing for home in foreign
lands spread the bush across alien corn.
Even on the bus between Sienna
and Rome, I saw yellow shrub shout from hills.
Invaders north and south. Insidious
brilliance first seducing then conquering,
roots grabbing death-grip. I've chopped, mowed, unearthed–
gouged hard with boot heel. I've poured my poison–
secret hearts burning in deadly feeding.
But dormant in the soil the seed lives years,
always promising the world to return.
I'll take what it knows, glean old wisdom
from such teaching: *hold on hold tight hold on.*

Some adults with insomnia

are afraid of the dark,
which resembles Snakemouth,
orchid with solitary rose-purple flower.
In the dark, 2.5 times more plastic

floats in the ocean
than anyone realizes, Spanish
researchers discover the place
where Caesar was stabbed, and bats
everywhere avoid moonlight.

Oh, sleepless the world's too much
with us. We twist
in our sheets, blankets bunched,
pillows flipped, clocks flashing.
Dwarf galaxy NGC consuming a smaller

dwarf galaxy, how Blake thought birds caged
and hanging in windows were metaphors
for people. All night we watch light
that took 13 billion years to reach earth

where Scalabrini's noseless lemur
is found to be a fish,
mosquito fossils glow in amber.
Did Otzi the ice mummy meet death

in the Alps over 5300 years ago because
of Lyme disease? How under Chairman Mao
The Fragrance of Sweet Wind restaurant
was renamed The Whiff of Gunpowder.

The Dam Tourist

The Grand Canyon of color
is a mere crack in the earth
entered in error in the tourists' guide
to hear him tell it.

He's held me at this party
too long bragging up
his last vacation west, a lead-in
where what he liked most
was Hoover Dam big and beautiful
dug from land and desert
by men last but not least
of God's minions, their mission
building dams and Mount Rushmore–

his other love, roster and rock
of presidents. The onus on me
to agree with this–

that floodlights through the night
focusing on the fluff
stirred by The Star-Spangled fuss
means never a dry eye.

But I keep sifting back
to canyon, curving crashing
river of copper, shift
of riprap under my boots, gorge
boggling this human blather,
this human hype, Lonely Planet hack.

Even seeing sunset
singing red from the rock
rendered his displeasure–
"No slam dunk, no big deal"
the seduction a bust.
"What's there to do out here?"
his tombstone's *mot juste*.

Bus Fare: A Pantoum

> *After a while, humanity*
> *wears on you.*
>   *—Toronto transit driver*

"Don't *crowd* the front. Move to the *back* of the bus."
We weren't exactly a boatload of lambs.
Barbed-wire music from earbuds,
we'd pound doors as you escaped curbs.

We weren't exactly a boatload of lambs,
your route schedule set at Central Control.
We'd pound doors as you escaped curbs,
and we'd out-fox as we faked transfer tickets,

your route schedule set at Central Control.
How even the doors hissed,
and we'd out-fox as we faked transfer tickets.
You were a run-down rental by shift's end—

how even the doors hissed.
City full of us wanting to be somewhere else,
you were a run-down rental by shift's end,
cars complaining as you squeezed lanes—

city full of us wanting to be somewhere else.
Coins clanking down the throat of the box,
cars complaining as you squeezed lanes,
diesel lungs of tractor trailers.

Coins clanking down the throat of the box,
barbed-wire music from earbuds,
diesel lungs of tractor trailers.
"Don't crowd the *front. Move* to the back of the bus."

In and Out of Sight

after the Column "Table for Two," The New Yorker

My companion and I are shown to a hand-woven table
in this dining establishment inspired by interiors of yachts

that have docked in too many cruise-coves in the tropics,
the menu offering elegant fare with a torchlight
complement flickering stucco walls

recalling vague memories of a philosophy class
that had to do with a cave in Greece and shadows
of passersby wafting in and out of sight,

significance of this

and the textbook long sold back to the bookstore

when our appetizer appeared–

choice tongue of now song-less yellow-breasted bunting
marinated in sauce from beluga lentils, end organs of taste

(the bunting's) excellently braised over imported charcoal
of cypress with hint of sanguine and where peppery nubs

(again, the bunting's)

rested unobtrusively in our mouths (forty dollars)

but the second appetizer
emerged before the tang of tongue had vanished, and we
wished the server had been more mindful of this breach
of cuisine, but no matter–

garlic-glazed black paw of ferret seared in scallion,
culmination of life slipping through keyholes–
while we savored clicking of claws artfully steamed
in ceci neri

sliding our throats, subtle flavor of forest and meadow

(fifty dollars) and not wanting to disappoint our anticipation
of the entrée, we resisted (with regrets) eye of sea turtle
served on slivers of almond topped with makrut lime,
but all told

it was too difficult to ignore this blend of brine and time

pierced with saffron that turned out to our delight to bring
last days of this creature to table (sixty dollars)

but the *piece de resistance* was worthy

of the buttery platter on which it rested: ruby-roasted heart
of Atlantic Puffin on a bed of oil glistening in the spark
of the shuttered bird

where we admired this creation
encrusted with fresh basil and curry leaf

(one hundred dollars)

and thinking to decline dessert, we found we could not,
our server displaying a pudding of white rhino milk
elegantly topped with the last visage of whipped cream.

Brother Rat

We decide to clear
the biggest fir that leans toward the house
and roots the drain field, crown dying for years,
boughs where the barred owl surveys comings and goings.

In September the squirrel leaped the tree,
needles ticking, snatched cones like someone
packing in a hurry. Our neighbor ties a rope on the trunk
tightening a knot on the bumper of his pickup,
cuts a notch and a deeper notch, wedge chunk free,
pulls the tree down to its landing place. All morning
I pile firewood and branches, cones littering the yard,
everything open to harm.

That night a thud on the planks of the porch.
Rat, the roar you raised—
your plague fleas, all you mean to king and dolt, your teeth
on the world. So we fired where you crouched
in your brown suit dangling your long hands
loose as candle flame, piano hands if one of our kind.

You're too much a fall from grace, cry-down gnaw
of rope and seed.
                      But we killed a wood rat—
trees and grass and fields, a stick-nest home.

Wrong blood to blame, no swamp, seaport, sewer.
How you bank bright things we leave and weave them
in your hut, live free from us. Prowl and spy to see
how we do, as close to us as we are far from you.

Consider the Dung Beetle

after Scarabacus sacer, Festooned
by Russ Weicking

Consider the dung beetle
rolling its world,
teaching the young
to make the best
from what's given.

How ancient Egyptians praised
scarab as an insect god
busy with important things—
driving the sun's rising & setting
& sweetening this life.

Her curiosity crumples

our chicken wire clamped on posts sunk nine
inches as she swaggers through, stripping oregano
to the root and shoots of dwarf peas–this cow
out of season where she isn't dropping
a calf, wife to no one, acting against
nature of cows, no anchoring elk-ardor
rutting–she's popping wire, ripping parsley,
hot manure plopped on raised beds in the ruined
garden, and as the fence falls, summer falls,
ravaged by cloven hoof, eradicated
by jaw, her battle with bitter weeds, spikes
of stinging bramble...over. Her relish
for tomatoes and apples and sweet corn.
Like Eve in her predicament, forever spoiled.

Speciesism

> *But I can see the cruelty / of something blindly dying,*
> *And I rush to intervene, imitatio dei.*
>   *—Karen Whalley, "Descent"*

Frying rockfish, I watch a spider zip toward the burner where
I swat it from the spatter of oil, crush it on the counter
with a paper towel.

At the Global Strike against Climate Change
a young woman blares into a loudspeaker, toddler on her hip.
She's teaching us a chorus as we wind down Front Street
past the Draughts and Arts Festival where tourists lift eyes
from phones, distracted by our hubble. Draped in blue sheets,
some of us bobble signs

> *Save the Orcas and Live Simply*
> *So Earth Can Simply Live*

My neighbor drives past in a dump truck from his day's work,
two boys in a Ford 350 gun us with carbon, middle fingers
skyward like horns from each window. There's some honking,
some woman waving from a smart car,
some voice roaring "Get a job!" while a man on a bicycle
herds us with a chant we're supposed to be chanting–

> *The Earth is crying, people are dying,*
> *justice for all species!*

It feels too much like high school football rallies
"Two four six eight   who do we appreciate? Terry! Donnie!
John!" which later became "One two three four
we don't want your fucking war!"

We straggle. We jam up at red lights. Most of us past
childbearing, we're no longer of use to biology,
our macrophages mauling our cells.

This spider descending toward my fish and feeding from
its web–for once it would be good to rearrange the small
cruelties of this world, open my hand to save.
But what of the ebony ant wrapped in spider silk?

Earth Song

What a glutted pantry you are, seeds, fruit,
fish and fowl, flesh—a goat's horn of plenty—
puma crushing windpipes of grazing deer,
brown bear slashing moose for the gleam-rich blood.
And this sirloin of pig we take from fire
sizzling, juices running clear. Once we lived
downwind from shoats until their eating life
erupted, bodies corn-fed inflated,
no room in the shed to lie down. Two men
flogging them up planks into trucks, hauling
stench and sorrow away. To live is to kill—
even tomatoes forfeit their future,
and when the sun devours planets and moons,
you'll know, too, what it is to be consumed.

~

Between the Blood Wolf Moon and this hot star
that neither speaks nor listens, this hour's
embossed with loss of light. So Mercury,
Venus, Earth. Jupiter, Saturn, Uranus.
Neptune with wayward Pluto forever
undone. Among the dark rocks and morning
star's navigation, red Mars under two
moons, Jupiter's ammonia clouds boiling.
A man without shelter in Seattle—
"I've had ammonia twice this winter,"
campfires flickering under freeway bridges
while Saturn spins ice, holding a wheat sheaf.
Among hydrogen methane, our blue-green
life never tilting in light this way again.

Notes on the Poems

"Life Drawing"
Alice Neel rendered her models as human beings as opposed to
ideals of human beings. Neel also painted new territory regarding
the nude study of the aging body, especially how women were
portrayed.

"After 'Nightmare'"
Dupree Bolton, 1929–1993

> "His sound was strong and brilliant, his attack swift and
> bright. The notes swarmed out of his horn …. He tended to
> come out of the gate already moving through the music at
> full speed, as if he thought there was no time to waste …. He
> died with nothing, with no family or friends on hand to mourn
> him."
>
> > "Gifted," *Granta 69*
> > Richard Williams

"Choose Your Own"
Eli "Lucky" Thompson, 1924-2005

Homeless in Seattle for decades,

> "a highly philosophical, almost mystical man, he eventually
> turned his back on the music business …. The real *tour de
> force* is the unaccompanied "Choose Your Own" …. Thompson
> never believed he had even scratched the surface in his career,
> a statement denied by the vivid and intense improvisation ….
> The sorry tailpiece to the story [a symposium planned to honor
> him] is that [it] was cancelled due to lack of interest."
>
> > *The Penguin Guide to Jazz Recordings, Ninth Edition*
> > Richard Cook and Brian Morton

"His Walden" is for Paula and Mike.

"Like Colored Glass: A Cento"
Thanks to Holly J. Hughes, who inspired this collage poem from
"Each Bird Singing: A Cento" from her poetry collection *Hold Fast.*

Poets in the order presented:

"The First Sunday of Hunting Season" and *"Via Negativa"*:
    Jude Nutter
"Trees": Galway Kinnell
Wen Fu ("The Art of Writing"): Lu Chi
"Epilogue": Robert Lowell
"Sunflower Sutra": Allen Ginsberg
"Ah, Sunflower": William Blake
"Kayaks": Henri Cole
"anyone lived in a pretty how town": E. E. Cummings

"So Much of War"
PTSD affects those who serve in a combat zone, all wars being the
same war, whether people are cooks, combatants, or ordnance as
was my father, who finally told me—when he was ninety—of his
trauma during WW II: "I thought I was weak," he said, referring to
overwhelming sadness that caused him sometimes to weep at the
end of a work day. I believe he felt that way until he died because
he never understood the true cause of his grief, how he referred to
the deaths he witnessed by saying, "It really bothered some guys,
but it really didn't bother me."

Tim Madigan writes in his piece "Their War Ended 70 Years Ago,
Their Trauma Didn't":

> "They talked of night terrors, heavy drinking, survivor's
> guilt, depression, exaggerated startle responses, profound and

lingering sadness. The symptoms were familiar to the world
by then, but post-traumatic stress disorder, the diagnosis
that came into being in 1980, was widely assumed to
be unique to veterans of Vietnam .... Those of age in the
late 1940s would have known differently.... But with the
passage of time and the prevailing male ethos–the strong,
silent type–World War II was soon overshadowed by the
Cold War and eventually Vietnam. By the 1990's, amid the
mythology of the Greatest Generation, the psychological
costs of the last 'good war' had been forgotten."

The Washington Post, 11 September 2015

"The Counterfeiters"
Han van Meegeren, 1889-1947

Jonathan Lopez writes in his book *The Man Who Made Vermeers*:

"His artistic frustration was that as a conservative artist
emulating the Old Masters, he wasn't celebrated. While
he made large sums of money painting portraits of the
aristocracy of Europe, he wanted greater wealth; a Dutch
fascist, his patrons included Goering. Van Meegeren was
brought to trial for forgery after the war, but Netherlanders
saw him as a folk hero who successfully conned Hitler's
minions. People didn't much care that he was a Hitler
supporter–or chose not to believe this about him. When
Goering was interviewed by a psychologist at Nuremburg
after the war, the Nazi referred to another kind of deception:
'The people can always be brought to the bidding of the
leaders. That is easy. All you have to do is tell them they are
being attacked and then denounce the pacifists for lack of
patriotism and exposing the country to danger. It works the
same in any country.'"

"The Evil Counsellors, The Despots" is dedicated to the
Ukrainian people.

The vignettes are based on Eugenia Ginzburg's powerful memoir
Journey into the Whirlwind, which contains phrases that are
disturbingly familiar in the current political environment of the
U.S. and the world. For example, those in opposition to Stalin and
his commissars were referred to as "enemies of the people," and
foremost among these "enemies" were journalists.

"Bus Fare" is for Michael Spence, who was a Seattle bus driver
for thirty years. He recounts his adventures in his poetry
collection *The Bus Driver's Threnody*.

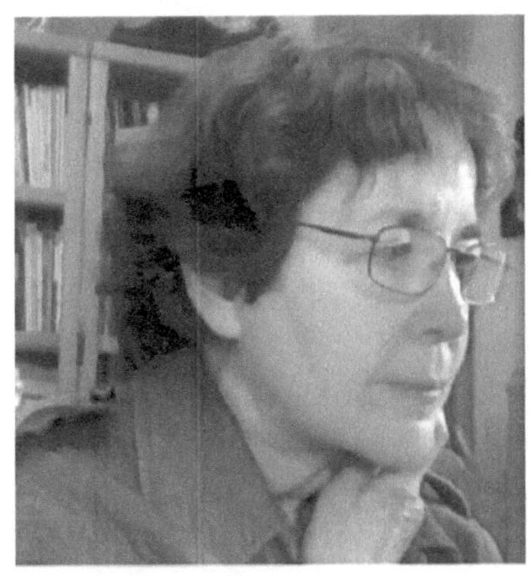

About the Author

Holding degrees in literature from the University of California, Santa Cruz, and the University of British Columbia, Carmen Germain is the author of the chapbook *Living Room, Earth* (Pathwise Press), the collections *These Things I Will Take with Me* (Cherry Grove), and *The Old Refusals* (MoonPath Press). Poems have appeared in various anthologies, including *In a Fine Frenzy: Poets Respond to Shakespeare* (University of Iowa Press), and *New Poets of the American West* (Many Voices Press). *Fifth Wednesday, The Madison Review, Cold Mountain Review, Poet Lore, Natural Bridge*, and *Flyway*, among others, have published her work. While on sabbatical as a visiting artist/scholar at the American Academy in Rome, she researched the work of the post-war novelist Elsa Morante.

She grew up near the Mississippi in rural Wisconsin and worked in Washington, D.C., Montana, and California before making her home in the Elwha River valley, Olympic Peninsula. She taught at Peninsula College, Port Angeles, for over twenty years where she was a co-director of the Foothills Writers Series. For parts of summers for thirty years she and her husband, Tom, lived in northern British Columbia in the river region of the Kispiox,

Skeena, and Babine with its grizzly and black bear, moose, and wolves. The South San Juan mountains of Colorado and Ajijic, Jalisco, Mexico, also influence her work.

James Bertolino writes of *The Old Refusals*: "Germain probes the natural world, the social world, the emotional world, and history in her poems. While she respects what she attends to, there is no such thing as a 'hands-off approach.' There are passages that glow with integrity, as well as those that flip known things over." Also an art maker who draws and paints, she agrees with Jorie Graham, who uses art to develop a poem: "I draw to keep the act of looking physical ... so you're not looking with your brain."

9 781936 657681

www.ingramcontent.com/pod-product-compliance
Lightning Source LLC
Chambersburg PA
CBHW021130070726
47591CB00014B/2082